HEALING FROM
the Scriptures

Bible Verses for Reading, Reciting, and Prayer

Norman H. Lyons, Jr.

HEALING FROM
the Scriptures

Bible Verses for Reading, Reciting, and Prayer

Norman H. Lyons, Jr.

*Formatted and Published by
NuVision Publishing*
www.nuvisiondesigns.biz

Copyright © 2020 Norman H. Lyons, Jr.
All rights reserved.

No part of ***Healing From the Scriptures*** may be used or reproduced by any means, graphic, electronic, or mechanical, including photocopying, recording, taping or by any information storage retrieval system without the written permission of the author except in the case of brief quotations embodied in critical articles and reviews.

Scriptures references are taken from the
KING JAMES VERSION (KJV),
public domain.

Books may be ordered by contacting:
Norman H. Lyons, Jr.
P.O. Box 86
Uniondale NY 11553

ISBN 978-1-5136-6221-3

PO Box 4455 | Wilmington NC
www.nuvisiondesigns.biz

Printed in the United States of America.

HEALING FROM THE SCRIPTURES

Introduction	7
Old Testament Scriptures	13
New Testament Scriptures	19
Scriptures for Your Health	45
The ABC's of Salvation	49
A Prayer for Salvation	51
Biographical Sketch of the Author	59

Introduction

Many years ago, a young minister that I grew up with was matriculating through Rhema Bible Training Institute. One night he called me and shared with me an amazing testimony about a healing course he was taking. He said, "I never knew there were so many healing scriptures in the Bible." He continued on to explain that as a result of reading so many healing scriptures as homework, he was healed of everything that was wrong with him. And in addition, he lost weight.

He said he didn't do anything extraordinary except read the healing scriptures he was assigned as homework. I never forgot that testimony, I treated it as a valued treasure. I am godly proud to say that now my friend Pastor Kevin L. Felder, along with his wife Vera, are the founders and pastors of the New Covenant Outreach Ministries in Greensboro, North Carolina.

About a decade later, my Chief Apostle and spiritual father Apostle Samuel Thomas of Sanford, North Carolina was suffering with some illnesses that required he take about 20 pills a day. He said the Lord spoke to him and told him to start reading 21 healing scriptures each day. He reported that as he heeded that word, he went from 20 pills down to 1 or 2 pills per day. His testimony reminded me of my friend's testimony, so I knew there was a significant correlation.

Fast forward to the fall and winter of 2019/2020. The Lord impressed upon me to start teaching a healing series at our local church. One of the principals I shared was the discipline of reading healing scriptures daily like a regular dosage of medication. I constantly repeated the two testimonies of my friend and my Apostle throughout the series.

The Lord directed me to lead our local church into a 9-month consecration. We gathered in the lobby of our church on monday nights for prayer. After 6 months, the coronavirus broke out and devastated the New York region where our church is located. However, at the beginning of the prayer consecration, the Lord said, by the time the consecration is over "The world will be changed, but you will be ahead of it."

And that is exactly what happened. At the time of this writing, the state is on "Shut Down." We are not allowed to congregate inside our building for worship as normal. We have been asked to conduct our services by live stream, facebook, or by phone.

As we are in the 7th month of our 9-month consecration, it seemed appropriate for me to write a mini-book of healing scriptures. This compilation of healing scriptures is intended to be a convenient ready reference for reading, reciting, and prayer. It is our hope that the readers will be renewed in the spirit of their minds to receive the healing God has promised in His word.

Old Testament
Healing Scriptures

Job 5:18 - For he maketh sore, and bindeth up: he woundeth, and his hands make whole.

Job 33:25 - His flesh shall be fresher than a child's: he shall return to the days of his youth.

Psalm 103:3 - Who forgiveth all thine iniquities; who healeth all thy diseases;

Isaiah 35:6 - Then shall the lame man leap as an hart, and the tongue of the dumb sing: for in the wilderness shall waters break out, and streams in the desert.

Exodus 15:26 - And said, If thou wilt diligently hearken to the voice of the Lord thy God, and wilt do that which is right in his sight, and wilt give ear to his commandments, and keep all his statutes, I will put none of these diseases upon thee, which I have brought upon the Egyptians: for I am the Lord that healeth thee.

Psalm 105:37 - He brought them forth also with silver and gold: and there was not one feeble person among their tribes.

Proverbs 4:20-22 – *(20)* My son, attend to my words; incline thine ear unto my sayings.

(21) Let them not depart from thine eyes; keep them in the midst of thine heart.

(22) For they are life unto those that find them, and health to all their flesh.

Isaiah 38:16 - O Lord, by these things men live, and in all these things is the life of my spirit: so wilt thou recover me, and make me to live.

Jeremiah 30:17 - For I will restore health unto thee, and I will heal thee of thy wounds, saith the Lord; because they called thee an Outcast, saying, This is Zion, whom no man seeketh after.

Daniel 1:15 - And at the end of ten days their countenances appeared fairer and fatter in flesh than all the children which did eat the portion of the Kings meat.

Isaiah 53:4-5 – *(4)* Surely he hath borne our grief's, and carried our sorrows: yet we did esteem him stricken, smitten of God, and afflicted.

(5) But he was wounded for our transgressions, he was bruised for our iniquities: the chastisement of our peace was upon him; and with his stripes we are healed.

Deuteronomy 7:15 - And the Lord will take away from thee all sickness, and will put none of the evil diseases of Egypt, which thou knowest, upon thee; but will lay them upon all them that hate thee.

New Testament Healing Scriptures

Mark 3:15 - And to have power to heal sicknesses, and to cast out devils.

Matthew 10:1 - And when he had called unto him his twelve disciples, he gave them power against unclean spirits, to cast them out, and to heal all manner of sickness and all manner of disease.

Mark 16: 18 - They shall take up serpents; and if they drink any deadly thing, it shall not hurt them; they shall lay hands on the sick, and they shall recover.

Matthew 4: 23 - And Jesus went about all Galilee, teaching in their synagogues, and preaching the gospel of the kingdom, and healing all manner of disease among the people.

Matthew 8:3 - And Jesus put forth his hand, and touched him, saying, I will; be thou clean. And immediately his leprosy was cleansed.

Matthew 8:16 - When the even was come, they brought unto him many that were possessed with devils: and he cast out the spirits with his word, and healed all that were sick:

Matthew 9:35 - And Jesus went about all the cities and villages, teaching in their synagogues, and preaching the gospel of the kingdom, and healing every sickness and every disease among the people.

Matthew 12:13 - Then saith he to the man, Stretch forth thine hand. And he stretched it forth; and it was restored whole, like as the other.

Matthew 14:36 - And besought him that they might only touch the hem of his garment: and as many as touched were made perfectly whole.

Matthew 15: 30 - And great multitudes came unto him, having with them those that were lame, blind, dumb, maimed, and many others, and cast them down at Jesus feet; and he healed them:

Matthew 17:18 - And Jesus rebuked the devil; and he departed out of him: and the child was cured from that very hour.

Matthew 19:2 - And great multitudes followed him; and he healed them there.

Matthew 21:14 - And the blind and the lame came to him in the temple; and he healed them.

Mark 1:31 - And he came and took her by the hand, and lifted her up; and immediately the fever left her, and she ministered unto them.

Mark 3: 1-5 – *(1)* And he entered again into the synagogue; and there was a man there which had a withered hand.

(2) And they watched him, whether he would heal him on the sabbath day; that they might accuse him.

(3) And he saith unto the man which had the withered hand, Stand forth.

(4) And he saith unto them, Is it lawful to do good on the sabbath days, or to do evil? to save life, or to kill? But they held their peace.

(5) And when he had looked round about on them with anger, being grieved for the hardness of their hearts, he saith unto the man, Stretch forth thine hand. And he stretched it out: and his hand was restored whole as the other.

Mark 3:10 - For he had healed many; insomuch that they pressed upon him for to touch him, as many as had plagues.

Mark 3:13-15 - *(13)* And he goeth up into a mountain, and calleth unto him whom he would: and they came unto him.

(14) And he ordained twelve, that they should be with him, and that he might send them forth to preach,

(15) And to have power to heal sicknesses, and to cast out devils:

Mark 5:27-29 - (27) When she had heard of Jesus, came in the press behind, and touched his garment.

(28) For she said, If I may touch but his clothes, I shall be whole.

(29) And straightway the fountain of her blood was dried up; and she felt in her body that she was healed of that plague.

Mark 6:4-5 - (4) But Jesus said unto them, A prophet is not without honour, but in his own country, and among his own kin, and in his own house.

(5) And he could there do no mighty work, save that he laid his hands upon a few sick folk, and healed them.

Mark 6:12-13 - *(12)* And they went out, and preached that men should repent.

(13) And they cast out many devils, and anointed with oil many that were sick, and healed them.

Mark 10: 52 - And Jesus said unto him, Go thy way; thy faith hath made thee whole. And immediately he received his sight, and followed Jesus in the way.

Luke 5:15 - But so much the more went there a fame abroad of him: and great multitudes came together to hear, and to be healed by him of their infirmities.

Luke 6:17-19 - (17) And he came down with them, and stood in the plain, and the company of his disciples, and a great multitude of people out of all Judaea and Jerusalem, and from the sea coast of Tyre and Sidon, which came to hear him, and to be healed of their diseases;

(18) And they that were vexed with unclean spirits: and they were healed.

(19) And the whole multitude sought to touch him: for there went virtue out of him, and healed them all.

Luke 7:20-21 - *(20)* When the men were come unto him, they said, John Baptist hath sent us unto thee, saying, Art thou he that should come? or look we for another?

(21) And in that same hour he cured many of their infirmities and plagues, and of evil spirits; and unto many that were blind he gave sight.

Luke 8:1-2 - (1) And it came to pass afterward, that he went throughout every city and village, preaching and shewing the glad tidings of the kingdom of God: and the twelve were with him,

(2) And certain women, which had been healed of evil spirits and infirmities, Mary called Magdalene, out of whom went seven devils,

Luke 9:1-2 - (1) Then he called his twelve disciples together, and gave them power and authority over all devils, and to cure diseases.

(2) And he sent them to preach the kingdom of God, and to heal the sick.

Luke 9:11 - And the people, when they knew it, followed him: and he received them, and spake unto them of the kingdom of God, and healed them that had need of healing.

Luke 9:41-42 - *(41)* And Jesus answering said, O faithless and perverse generation, how long shall I be with you, and suffer you? Bring thy son hither.

(42) And as he was yet a coming, the devil threw him down, and tare him. And Jesus rebuked the unclean spirit, and healed the child, and delivered him again to his father.

Luke 13:10-13 - (10) And he was teaching in one of the synagogues on the Sabbath.

(11) And, behold, there was a woman which had a spirit of infirmity eighteen years, and was bowed together, and could in no wise lift up herself.

(12) And when Jesus saw her, he called her to him, and said unto her, Woman thou art loosed from thine infirmity.

(13) And he laid his hands on her: and immediately she was made straight, and glorified God.

Luke 14: 2-4 - (2) And, behold, there was a certain man before him which had the dropsy.

(3) And Jesus answering spake unto the lawyers and Pharisees, saying, Is it lawful to heal on the sabbath day?

(4) And they held their peace. And he took him, and healed him, and let him go;

Luke 17:12-14 - *(12)* And as he entered into a certain village there met him ten men that were lepers, which stood afar off:

(13) And they lifted up their voices, and said, Jesus, Master, have mercy on us.

(14) And when he saw them, he said unto them, Go shew yourselves unto the priests. And it came to pass, that, as they went, they were cleansed.

Luke 22:50-51 - *(50)* And one of them smote the servant of the high priest, and cut off his right ear.

(51) And Jesus answered and said, Suffer ye thus far. And he touched his ear, and healed him.

John 5:8-9 - *(8)* Jesus saith unto him, Rise, take up thy bed, and walk.

(9) And immediately the man, was made whole, and took up his bed, and walked: and on the same day was the sabbath.

Acts 3:6-11 - *(6)* Then Peter said, Silver and gold have I none; but such as I have give I thee: In the name of Jesus Christ of Nazareth rise up and walk.

(7) And he took him by the right hand, and lifted him up: and immediately his feet and ankle bones received strength.

(8) And he leaping up stood, and walked, and entered with them into the temple, walking, and leaping, and praising God.

(9) And all the people saw him walking and praising God:

(10) And they knew that it was he which sat for alms at the Beautiful gate of the temple: and they were filled with wonder and amazement at that which had happened unto him.

(11) And as the lame man which was healed held Peter and John, all the people ran together unto them in the porch that is called Solomon's, greatly wondering.

Acts 3:16 - And his name through faith in his name hath made this man strong, whom ye see and know: yea, the faith which is by him hath given him this perfect soundness in the presence of you all.

Acts 4:13-14 - *(13)* Now when they saw the boldness of Peter and John, and perceived that they were unlearned and ignorant men, they marvelled; and they took knowledge of them, that they had been with Jesus.

(14) And beholding the man which was healed standing with them, they could say nothing against it.

Acts 5:12-16 - *(12)* And by the hands of the apostles were many signs and wonders wrought among the people; (and they were all with one accord in Solomon's porch.

(13) And of the rest durst no man join himself to them: but the people magnified them.

(14) And believers were the more added to the Lord, multitudes both of men and women.)

(15) Insomuch that they brought forth the sick into the streets, and laid them on beds and couches, that at the least the shadow of Peter passing by might overshadow some of them.

(16) There came also a multitude out of the cities round about unto Jerusalem, bringing sick folks, and them which were vexed with unclean spirits: and they were healed every one.

Acts 8:5-8 - *(5)* Then Philip went down to the city of Samaria, and preached Christ unto them.

(6) And the people with one accord gave heed unto those things which Philip spake,

hearing and seeing the miracles which he did.

(7) For unclean spirits, crying with loud voice, came out of many that were possessed with them: and many taken with palsies, and that were lame, were healed.

(8) And there was great joy in the city.

Acts 14:7-10 - *(7)* And there they preached the gospel.

(8) And there sat a certain man at Lystra, impotent in his feet, being a cripple from his mother's womb, who never had walked:

(9) The same heard Paul speak: who stedfastly beholding him, and perceiving that he had faith to be healed,

(10) Said with a loud voice, Stand upright on thy feet. And he leaped and walked.

Acts 28:8-9 - *(8)* And it came to pass, that the father of Publius lay sick of a fever and of a bloody flux: to whom Paul entered in, and prayed, and laid his hands on him and healed him.

(9) So when this was done, others also, which had diseases in the island, came, and were healed:

I Corinthians 12:9 -To another faith by the same Spirit; to another the gifts of healing by the same Spirit;

I Corinthians 12:30 - Have all the gifts of healing? do all speak with tongues? do all interpret?

James 5:14-15 - *(14)* Is any sick among you? let him call for the elders of the church; and let them pray over him, anointing him with oil in the name of the Lord.

(15) And the prayer of faith shall save the sick, and the Lord shall raise him up; and if he have committed sins, they shall be forgiven him.

I Peter 2:24 - Who his own self bare our sins in his own body on the tree, that we, being dead to sins, should live unto righteousness: by whose stripes ye were healed.

Scriptures for Your Health

III John 2 - Beloved, I wish above all things that thou mayest prosper and be in health, even as thy soul prospereth.

Genesis 43:28 - And they answered, Thy servant our father is in good health, he is yet alive. And they bowed down their heads, and made obeisance.

Psalm 42:11 - Why art thou cast down, O my soul? And why art thou disquieted within me? hope thou in God; for I shall yet praise him, who is the health of my countenance, and my God.

Psalm 67:1-2 - (1) God be merciful unto us, and bless us; and cause his face to shine upon us; Selah.

(2) That thy way may be known upon earth, thy saving health among all nations.

Proverbs 3:7-8 - (7) Be not wise in thine own eyes: fear the Lord, and depart from evil.

(8) It shall be health to thy navel, and marrow to thy bones.

Proverbs 12-18 - There is that speaketh like the piercings of a sword: but the tongue of the wise is health.

Proverbs 16:24 - Pleasant words are as an honeycomb, sweet to the soul, and health to the bones.

Isaiah 58:8 -Then shall thy light break forth as the morning, and thine health shall spring forth speedily: and thy righteousness shall go before thee; the glory of the Lord shall be thy rereward.

The ABC's of Salvation

A. **Admit that you have sinned.** "For all have sinned, and come short of the glory of God." *(Romans 3:23)*

B. Believe on Jesus Christ the Savior. "For God so loved the world, that he gave his only begotten Son, that whosoever Believeth in Him should not perish, but have everlasting life." *(John 3:16)*

C. Confess. "That if thou shalt confess with thy mouth the Lord Jesus and shalt believe in thine heart that God hath raised him from the dead, thou shalt be saved, For with the heart man believeth unto righteousness; and with the mouth confession is made unto salvation." *(Romans 10: 9-10)*

A Prayer for Salvation

"Heavenly Father in Jesus name, I confess that I am a sinner. Forgive me for my sin and save me. I repent of my sin. I believe in my heart on the Lord Jesus Christ and confess with my mouth that I accept Him as my personal Lord and Saviour. Thank you for saving me. Amen."

NOTES

NOTES

NOTES

NOTES

I trust that you have given your life to Christ.
As you apply the Word to your life
and continue to seek the Lord,
you will be richly blessed.

Norman H. Lyons, Jr.

Letters of Support can be sent to:
NORMAN LYONS, JR. MIN. INC.
PO Box 86
Uniondale NY 11553

BIOGRAPHICAL SKETCH OF THE AUTHOR

Bishop Norman Lyons, Jr. is the founder and senior pastor of the Fountain of Life Church in Uniondale, New York. In addition to his national ministry, he has also done missionary work in Haiti, Nigeria, West Africa and Italy. Bishop Lyons has served as an executive council member of the International Council of Local Churches. He has also served as a member of M.E.C.C.A. For seven years Bishop Lyons was a Board Member of the New York Call hosted by Pastor Donnie McClurkin. He is currently the Chaplain for the Long Island Conference of Clergy.

At the time of this writing, Bishop Lyons has been preaching for 41 years. He has been married to his darling wife, Pastor Sharon, for 40 years. They have pastored the Fountain of Life Church for 37 years.

Norman and Sharon are the grateful parents of two daughters, Juliet and Jasmine. They also have been blessed with a son-in-love, Joaquin, Juliet's husband.

www.ingramcontent.com/pod-product-compliance
Lightning Source LLC
Chambersburg PA
CBHW061513040426
42450CB00008B/1596